Hijack Over Hygenia

A Musical Play for Children

David Wood

A SAMUEL FRENCH ACTING EDITION

SAMUEL FRENCH

FOUNDED 1830

SAMUELFRENCH-LONDON.CO.UK
SAMUELFRENCH.COM

ISBN 978-0-573-05034-3

www.samuelfrench-london.co.uk

www.samuelfrench.com

FOR AMATEUR PRODUCTION ENQUIRIES

UNITED KINGDOM AND WORLD
EXCLUDING NORTH AMERICA
plays@SamuelFrench-London.co.uk
020 7255 4302/01

Each title is subject to availability from Samuel French,

depending upon country of performance.

HIJACK OVER HYGENIA

First produced at the Swan Theatre, Worcester, by the Worcester Repertory Company, on Boxing Day 1973, with the following cast of characters:

Pilot Hare, of United Hareways	Derek Snook
Gadget, odd job man and part inventor; elderly, well-meaning, prone to mistakes; short-sighted, wears spectacles	
Measle, an unpleasant germ; looks like a cross between a mouse and a weasel	Alex Johnston
Weathervane, vain revolving cockerel; superior though courageous	Robert Meadwell
Measlygerm Three, one of Measle's disease-spreading colleagues	
Aerial, a T.V. aerial who dabbles in science	Garth Spiers
Measlygerm Two	
King Spring of Hygenia, obsessed by the cleanliness of his Kingdom; pompous, cowardly, but respected	Giles Phibbs
Hare Plane Passenger	
Queen Clean of Hygenia, fat, chocolate-loving, bossy wife of King Spring	Sheila Irwin
Hare Plane Passenger	
Princess Spotless, plain, plaitted, whiny, bespectacled daughter of the King and Queen	Jacqui Dubin
Hare Plane Passenger	
Grime Minister, highest official of the Government of Hygenia, carries an ornate broom as staff of office	Leslie Glazer
Hare Plane Passenger	
Measlygerm One	
Stainless, the Cat, made of stainless steel for bravery, but now terrified of the untoward because Hygenia is so clean there are no mice or rats left. Should be played by a female	Helen Kluger
Hare Plane Passenger	
The Court Duster, new recruit to the Palace team. Supposed to tell clean jokes while polishing	John A. Cooper
Hare Plane Passenger	
Auntie Septic, an elderly aerosol spray, devoted to her duty to keep everything germ-free	Anna Nicholas
Hare Stewardess	
Doctor Spicknspan, mid-European hygiene expert attached to the Court	John Bleasdale
Hare Plane Passenger	

Directed by John Hole
Setting by Tony Leah

The play is set in and above the Kingdom of Hygenia, the Cleanest Place
in the World. By clever use of levels it should be possible to isolate the roof
of the Palace without changing the scene below. The Princess's bedroom set
should not impede the view of the roof.

MUSICAL NUMBERS

1. "Flying, Flying" **Pilot Hare, Hareplane Navigator, Hare Stewardess,**
Hareplane Passengers
2. "Up on This Roof Together" **Weathervane, Aerial**
3. "Hygenia" **King Spring, Queen Clean, Princess Spotless,**
Grime Minister, Duster, Gadget, Auntie Septic
4. "The Rocket Song" **Gadget**
4a. "The Rocket Song" (Reprise) **King Spring and the Court**
5. "Clean All Over" **Queen Clean, Auntie Septic, Princess Spotless**
6. "The Phone Message" **Aerial, Weathervane**
7. "I'm A Measle" **Measle**

INTERVAL

8. "The Princess Spotless is Spotty" **King Spring, Queen Clean,**
Grime Minister, Duster, Gadget and Auntie Septic
9. "It's the Fever!" **Doctor Spicknspan, King Spring and the Court**
9a. "The Rocket Song" (Reprise) **King Spring, Grime Minister,**
Doctor Spicknspan, Duster, Gadget, Auntie Septic
10. "Rumble, Rumble" **Gadget**
10a. "Rumble, Rumble" (Reprise) **Gadget**
10b "It's the Fever!" (Reprise) **Weathervane, Aerial**
10c. "The Princess Spotless is Spotty" (Reprise)
King Spring, Queen Clean, Princess Spotless
10d. "The Princess Spotless is Spotty" (Reprise)
Grime Minister and the Royal Family

The piano/vocal score is available from Samuel French Ltd

ACT I

PROLOGUE

As the members of the audience enter the auditorium, it should be as if they are boarding an aeroplane. Perhaps the usherettes could be dressed as stewardesses. At regular intervals we hear the "bing bong" noise heralding an announcement

Female Voice United Hareways announce the departure of Flight HA four-oh-one-six, the holiday special to Amnesia, passing over Hygenia, the Kingdoms of Cornucopia and Agraphobia. This flight is now boarding at Gate Five, and passengers are asked to take their seats as soon as possible. Thank you.

The announcement is repeated two or three times. As the Lights go down for the beginning of the play, another voice is heard, as well as the sounds of an aeroplane preparing for take-off

Second Female Voice Good afternoon, ladies and gentlemen, and on behalf of Captain Springer welcome aboard this United Hareways special holiday flight to Amnesia; we shall be flying over Hygenia, the Kingdoms of Cornucopia and Agraphobia, and light refreshments will be served. Now please fasten your seat belts for take-off. Thank you.

The Houselights black out and we hear the dramatic building roar of engines. The plane "takes off" and the CURTAIN *rises*

SCENE 1

Inside the Hareplane

Captain Springer, the Hare Pilot, and his Navigator are at the controls. Passengers sit in excitement. The Hare Stewardess serves the odd drink.

Song 1—FLYING, FLYING

All
Flying, Flying
Follow the swallows, high in the sky
Flying, flying
Watching the world below flash by.

Way up in the clouds
Away from the crowds
Far from the bustle and noise
The sea is so shiny
The mountains so tiny
The cars could be toys.

Flying, flying
Follow the swallows, high in the sky
Flying, flying
Watching the world below flash by.

Pilot	We climb and we climb	
Navigator	In very quick time	
Stewardess	Gasp at the beautiful view	*Singing*
	Who cares where we're going?	*together*
	We're going by Boeing	
	To cruise through the blue.	

All

Flying, flying
Follow the swallows, high in the sky
Flying, flying
Watching the world below flash by.

Stewardess

Tea or coffee
Coffee or tea
At your service
Just send for me
Snacks or sav'ries
Fresh from the grill
Barley sugar
If you feel ill

All

Flying, flying
Follow the swallows, high in the sky
Flying, flying
Watching the world below flash by
Waving the world below good-bye
Wondering how we got this high
What a great feeling—to fly.

The Hare Pilot takes the microphone

Hare Pilot Good afternoon, ladies and gentlemen. This is your Captain speaking. My, my, my, what a super-duper view you have of the crazy earth below. Doesn't it just blow your mind? Very soon you'll see the rooftops of Hygenia.

Navigator ⎱ (*like a TV commercial*) Hygenia, the ⎰ *Speaking*
Hare Pilot ⎰ cleanest Kingdom in the world. ⎱ *together*

Suddenly the Lights become very bright

Hare Pilot There it is! Wow! You can see the brightness!

A suspicious-looking character in a long coat and wide-brimmed hat stands up and advances to the cockpit area. He stands behind the Hare Pilot

Hare Pilot ⎱ Hygenia—cleaner than clean. Brighter than ⎰ *Speaking*
Navigator ⎰ white, whiter than . . . ⎱ *together*
Measle Hi-jack.

Hare Pilot Hi man. (*Carrying on*) Brighter than white . . .
Measle I said, Hi-jack.
Hare Pilot Hi man. Whiter than . . . Hey, why d'you call me Jack? My
    name's Harry.
Measle I didn't. (*He produces a gun*) I said HI-JACK.

The passengers overhear this. Consternation

Hare Pilot Oh my. (*He raises his arms above his head*)

*The plane lurches violently as the controls are abandoned. The Hare Pilot
grabs them again*

    (*Shaking violently*) O.K., O.K., so what do you want?
Measle (*addressing the whole plane*) Nobody move, and nobody'll get hurt.
Passengers (*jibbering together*)
                Who are you?
                How dare you?
                O Percy, I feel one of my spasms coming on.
                Let me get at him.
                Sit down you fool, etc., etc.

Measle lets them all see the gun. Stunned silence

Measle That's better. (*To the Hare Pilot*) What height are we?
Hare Pilot Navigator?
Navigator F-F-F-Four thousand feet.
Measle Circle and fly lower. Right over the King's Palace.

The Passengers gasp

Hare Pilot But you can't . . .

The gun stops him saying more.

    O.K., man, O.K., keep cool, keep cool. (*To the Navigator*) Do as he says.

The Hare Pilot gives the impression of circling. Music for tension

Navigator Three thousand five hundred. (*Pause*) Three thousand.
Hare Pilot (*to Measle*) You can just see the Palace now.
Measle Lower.
Navigator Two thousand feet.
Measle (*beckoning to the Stewardess with his gun*) You—get ready to open
    the door.
Stewardess But . . .
Measle Don't argue.
Navigator One thousand.
Measle (*looking out*) Is that it?
Hare Pilot Yes.

*Measle throws off his coat and hat, revealing his furry body, and a parachute
on his back*

Navigator Five hundred feet.

Measle grabs his suitcase

Measle Open up.

The Stewardess opens the door. Measle pulls the parachute and jumps. The Lights fade to a Black-Out. The roar of engines and music increases as the scene changes

SCENE 2

On the Palace roof

Being in Hygenia, even the roof is very clean. There are a chimney pot, telephone wires and connections, and an Aerial fixed near the pot. A Weathervane is fixed in a more exposed position—he can revolve, but not change position. They are spending a normal, quiet day. Weathervane speaks as he revolves this way and that. He rarely loses his temper, and speaks in a languid, toffee-nosed manner

Weathervane (*looking into the sky*) For heaven's sake, make your mind up.
Aerial (*hearing and "waking up"*) What's the matter, cock?
Weathervane This frightfully fickle wind! Ah! (*The wind catches him again and he changes position. He draws breath to recover*) It persists in changing direction with absolutely no warning. (*It does it again, violently*) Ah! Nor' nor' west, sou' sou' east. Much more of this indecision and I shall suffer an attack of the vapours.
Aerial Chin up, cock. All part of the job.
Weathervane Maybe. But nobody takes the blindest bit of notice of me, wherever I'm pointing. So what's the point of pointing in the first place?
Aerial But you're a personality, in permanent public view. In Hygenia there's only one weathercock, cock.
Weathervane The job has snob value, I grant you—and, er—Aerial, please refrain from referring to me as "cock". It's most vulgar. I'm a weather*vane*. I'm not "cock", I'm "vane". (*He preens himself*)
Aerial You're telling me, cock, I mean vane!

Song 2—UP ON THIS ROOF TOGETHER

Weathervane	I go where the wind blows
Aerial	I stay static
Weathervane	I'm controlled by elements
Aerial	And I am automatic
Weathervane	I send telly pictures
Both	I show weather
	Day in day out we're stuck
	Up on this roof together

                    Through rain or shine
                    We stand to attention
                    Through fair or fine
                    But we never get a mention.

                    Through hail and fog
                    Forlorn and forgotten
                    Through smoke and smog
                    'Cos the royal lot are rotten.

                    We can't move
                    From this solitary spot
Aerial   But I can just sway a bit
Weathervane (*feeling sick*) And I revolve a lot.

Both   Through ice and snow
                    It's not funny, is it?
                    It's years ago
                    Since we had a royal visit.

Weathervane   I go where the wind blows
Aerial   I stay static
Weathervane   I'm controlled by elements
Aerial   And I am automatic.
                    I send telly pictures
Weathervane   I show weather
Both   Day in day out we are stuck
                    Up on this roof together.

Weathervane What's on the telly, Aerial?

Aerial Hang on. I'll twiddle my knobs and tune in. (*He does so*)

Weathervane I'm just in the mood for something interesting and educational and erudite . . .

A voice comes from Aerial, increasing in volume as Weathervane speaks

Television Voice . . . don't be mistaken, don't be misled, don't miss the mystery ingredient missing from most washing powders—let Mister Sparkle put a sparkle on *your* washing up—Mister Sparkle, Hygenia's most popular . . .

Weathervane Turn off that trivial trashy tripe.

Aerial twiddles his knobs

It's ridiculous. There's nothing to do on this wretched roof. Nothing exciting ever happens, nothing . . .

Weathervane is interrupted by the sound of a low-flying aircraft. Both he and Aerial react to the increasing volume. Then the wind changes because of the plane. Aerial has to hang on to the roof for support. Weathervane turns helplessly round in circles. In their panic they catch sight of something above them, and watch

Measle lands on the roof (in or out of vision). He folds up his parachute as the noises of the plane fade

Aerial Are you all right?

No answer

Who are you?

No answer

Weathervane *What* are you? (*Scathingly*) Looks like a flying weasle.
Aerial Or a mouse.
Weathervane Ugh!

Measle moves threateningly towards Weathervane

Keep away, you horrid little creature.
Measle (*with no time to waste on trivialities*) This the Palace?
Aerial Yes. What do you want here?
Weathervane Filthy little beast. Vermin!
Aerial Sssh, Weathervane, please. (*To Measle*) I don't think you're meant
to be here, are you?
Measle Just visiting. (*He surveys the roof, finds the telephone wires and
examines them*)
Weathervane You can't stay here. This is Hygenia, the Cleanest Kingdom
in the World. No dirt, no disease for donkey's years.
Aerial It's true. Even I'm cleaned and polished every other day.
Weathervane They'll kick you out, and good riddance. (*He holds his nose*)
Pooh Aerial, I can smell him from here.

*Measle takes no notice. He is busily testing the wires, having opened his case
which contains instruments, etc. There is a sudden loud "bleep, bleep" sound
from Aerial*

Measle (*jumping*) What's that?
Aerial News flash. Hang on a tick. (*He twiddles his knobs*)
Measle What are you doing?
Aerial Just receiving the news flash and sending it down into the television
in the Palace.
Television Voice This is a news flash, a news flash. A low-flying aircraft
has just passed over Hygenia. At first it was thought the pilot was out of
control, but as the aeroplane passed over the King's Palace, it regained
height and flew on in apparent safety. That is the end of the news flash.

*Measle continues his business. He puts on headphones and attaches a dialling
apparatus to one of the telephone wires*

Aerial (*connecting Measle with the plane mentioned in the news flash*) Hey,
you bailed out of that low-flying aircraft, didn't you?

No reply

What are you up to?
Weathervane And what are you doing with those wires? Telephone tam-
pering is a serious offence.
Aerial (*getting annoyed*) If I could move, I'd . . .

Measle But you can't. Neither of you. You're stuck in one position. So shut up. (*He dials a number*)

We hear a faint ring below. It stops as someone the other end picks up the receiver

(*Into the mouthpiece*) Hallo. Boss?
Garbled unintelligible answers are heard throughout the conversation

M One-oh-one. Await confirmation of next move . . . Message understood . . . Over and out. (*He rings off and starts packing up his equipment*)
Aerial Now look here, I've had enough . . .

Measle takes no notice of Aerial, but carries on packing

Weathervane Don't speak to him. I won't. It's beneath my dignity.

Measle goes towards the chimney pot

Suddenly, Stainless the Cat appears

Measle stops in his tracks, for the first time frightened

Aerial It's Stainless!

Measle dashes behind the chimney pot

After him, Puss, there's a good boy. Teach him a lesson. Attack. Attack. (*In a robot voice*) M One-oh-one must be destroyed.

Stainless takes no notice, but walks normally past them, towards the other side

Huh, he's useless.
Weathervane It's not his fault. He's never seen a verminous creature, or if he *has*, Hygenia's so clean he's forgotten what they look like.

Measle emerges tentatively, and makes a sudden "Boo" movement to Stainless

Stainless exits, terrified
   Measle quickly climbs into the chimney pot and disappears from view

Aerial Hey! Where are you going? You can't go down there!

Aerial and Weathervane struggle at their moorings but are unable to stop Measle

Weathervane He's not worth the effort. There's nothing we can do.
Aerial But that chimney leads to the throne room.

There is an urgent "bleep, bleep" from Aerial. He tunes in quickly

Television Voice This is a news flash. The aircraft thought to be in difficulty over Hygenia has radioed that an enemy has been dropped over the Palace. He is described as of slight build, furry, and of a desperate character. He is armed, and though we have no news of his intentions in Hygenia, could well be dangerous.

There is a dramatic chord of music. Aerial and Weathervane look at each other. After a pause the Lights fade and music leads into the next scene

SCENE 3

The Throne Room in the Palace

It is very clean and functional. There are a fireplace, a television, a window, a clock and a telephone, plus, of course, thrones. The Court Duster sprawls, duster over his face, in a throne, snoring loudly. From off stage a female voice calls "Duster, Duster!" The Duster wakes violently and automatically polishes the throne with vehemence, muttering

Duster (*automatically*) Yes, your Majesty, no, your Majesty, sorry, your Majesty . . . (*Realizing no-one is there, he stops, and notices the audience. He comes forward to address them, not as an audience participation section so much as a friendly chat*) Oh. How do. I thought I heard the Queen. Real bossy, she is. She . . . Hang on, I'll tell you who I am first. I'm the new Court Duster. (*Confidentially*) They're having an economy drive—one person—me—two jobs—I make them laugh like a court jester, but I have to clean things at the same time. I get so tired. Anyway . . .

The voice off shouts "Duster"! Duster stops gossiping, and polishes

Auntie Septic enters

Auntie Septic Duster! There you are.
Duster Oh, it's you, Auntie Septic. Phew! (*Stopping work*) I thought it was Her Majesty.
Auntie Septic Well, don't stop polishing, Duster. They're on their way. It's almost time for the Royal Viewing. (*She goes to the television set and sprays it several times*)
Duster The Royal Viewing? (*Realizing*) Oh, the telly. (*Polishing it*) What's on?
Auntie Septic Oh, that serial, *Love in the Launderette*. It's a soap opera— it's a very clean programme.

Gadget enters in a nervous hurry

Gadget Here they come, here they come, here they come, here they come . . . (*He rushes round checking all is well, nearly knocking over the others, repeating "Here they come" over and over. He pushes the television into position before the thrones. Returning to Duster and Auntie Septic, he trips over the extended television flex, falls, is helped up, still muttering "Here they come". He sees Duster*) Here they come, here they come, who are you?
Auntie Septic This is the new Court Duster.

Gadget (*still recovering*) How do you do? Gadget. Odd jobs, inventions, television tuner and turner-oner.

A loud fanfare spurs them into final cleaning and polishing

Majestically, the Grime Minister leads in the Royal party, King Spring, Queen Clean and Princess Spotless

Duster, nudged on by Auntie Septic, polishes the ground before them, and Auntie Septic keeps up a regular spray to clean the air they are about to walk into

Song 3—HYGENIA

All	A kingdom of worth
	Hygenia
	A kingdom of mirth
	Hygenia
	Of dirt there's a dearth
	It's the cleanest kingdom on earth
	The kingdom of our birth
	Hygenia
Auntie Septic	No dirty things like toads
	In Hygenia
Grime Minister	We vacuum all the roads
	In Hygenia
King	We gargle ev'ry hour
Queen	We polish every flower
All	And after meals we have a shower
	In Hygenia
King and Queen	We sterilize the meat
	In Hygenia
Auntie Septic	Deodorize the feet
	In Hygenia
Grime Minister	We disinfect the tea
Duster	We pasteurize the sea
All	So we are all bacteria-free
	In Hygenia
Gadget	A smoke's against the law
	In Hygenia
Princess Spotless	We eat off ev'ry floor
	In Hygenia
King and Queen	Our subjects don't have fleas
	Or die from a disease
Duster	They're out shampooing all the trees
All	In Hygenia
	A kingdom of worth
	Hygenia

A kingdom of mirth
Hygenia
Of dirt there's a dearth
It's the cleanest kingdom on earth
The kingdom of our birth
Hygenia.

At the end of the song the King and Queen sit on their thrones and talk animatedly with the Grime Minister. Gadget stands ready for action at the television, and Auntie Septic stands near the thrones ready to spray if required. Duster finishes dusting the base of the throne, under the royal couple's feet, then backs away. Princess Spotless, who has been sucking a large lollipop since arriving, neatly positions it on the floor. She trips up Duster, who falls backwards onto the sticky lolly. He yells out with surprise. Princess Spotless dashes behind the thrones. The King and Queen react to the yell

King What's that?
Queen (*constantly eating chocolates from a box held by the Grime Minister*) Who's that?

Duster is caught holding the lollipop

Grime Minister This, your Majesties, is the new Court Duster.
King Splendid.
Queen Make me laugh, Duster.

Clearly, little would make the Queen laugh. At this moment, Princess Spotless appears between the thrones, behind her parents, and, unseen by them, sticks out her tongue at Duster. He immediately makes a very rude face back. The royal couple react shocked

King How dare you!
Queen Rude fellow.
Duster But that horrid little girl stuck out . . .

Princess Spotless immediately puts on an innocent, regal face

Queen Our daughter is never horrid. She is beautiful.
King (*to the Queen*) Just like you, dear.
Queen She is charming.
King Just like you, dear.
Duster She's ugly and cheeky.
King Just like you, dear.
Queen (*furiously*) What?
King Oh, sorry, dear. Watch your tongue, Duster, or we will pick you up and shake you from the window. My daughter . . .

The Queen nudges the King

Our daughter, Princess Spotless, is never wrong.
Princess Spotless Can I have my lollipop?
King Yes, darling, how much do you want?
Princess No, not my lolly, pop—my lollipop—Duster's pinched it.

Queen Give it back at once, you brute.

Duster hands out the lollipop. Princess Spotless comes round to collect it. Duster backs away

King And in future stick to your job. Don't be rude; make us laugh.

Princess Spotless trips Duster up. All laugh

Queen Ha, ha. That's better.

Suddenly the clock chimes loudly. All stand to attention except Gadget, who nudges Duster

Gadget Psst. The glasses

Duster removes Gadget's spectacles and cleans them

No, no, no. The drinking glasses.

Duster rushes off

Grime Minister (*formally*) The Royal Gargle.

All clear their throats

Duster enters with a tray and hands out glasses

All in a routine manner gargle loudly, then drink. Duster collects up the glasses

Stainless the cat enters. He acts nervously
Duster takes the tray off and returns

Princess Spotless Stainless, what's the matter? She's warning us about something

Stainless tries to mime that something fishy and frightening has happened on the roof, when another fanfare stops everything

Grime Minister Your Majesties, King Spring, Queen Clean and Princess Spotless. The Court of Hygenia, represented by I myself, the Grime Minister, announce with pleasure it is time for—the Royal Viewing.

Cheers

Gadget, the switch.

Gadget moves formally and reverently towards the television. As he goes to turn it on there is a huge crash

Measle enters down the fireplace

There is a spray of soot. Consternation. Terror. Auntie Septic immediately starts spraying madly and urges Duster to polish too. Stainless tries to hide under Princess Spotless's skirt

Queen My train! etc. (*She picks it up and feverishly brushes it*)
Princess Spotless Stainless! It's all right. No-one's going to hurt you.
Grime Minister There's soot on my suit. Soot on my suit! Ahhh!
King Dirt! Dirt! Get rid of it, get rid of it!

Gadget runs to the fireplace to trace the trouble

  In the pandemonium, Measle manages to rush off unseen

  What's happening?
Gadget Something fell down the chimney, your Highness

  Gadget rushes off and returns with a dustpan and brush, and sweeps

King (*turning ferociously on Duster*) You! You're new. This must be your
  doing.
Queen You can never trust a duster! (*She eats chocolates*)
Grime Minister (*intervening*) Your Majesty, your Majesty, please. Duster
  had nothing to do with it. Allow me to fix the fireplace; Gadget will
  brick it in tomorrow.
King Very well. It's about time we had central heating.
Grime Minister Shall I turn on the television now, your Majesty?
Queen (*who has been eating even more, in her nervous state*) No, no, I
  couldn't watch in this state. And with all this dirt everywhere. (*She
  shudders*)
Princess Spotless It's all right, Stainless, stop shaking.
Gadget (*who by now has swept up most of the soot*) Your Majesty, might I
  take this opportunity of demonstrating my latest invention?
King But your inventions never work, Gadget.
Gadget Have no fear, your Majesty, this one does, and it'll help clean all
  this mess.
King Oh, very well then.

Gadget whispers to the Grime Minister, then starts to exit

Gadget (*to Duster*) Give us a hand, Duster.
Duster Right.

  Gadget and Duster exit

The Grime Minister steps forward. Fanfare

Grime Minister Your Majesties. Gadget proudly presents his Docket
  Raste Wisposal—er, Wocket Daste Sisposal—no, er . . .

*Gadget and Duster enter, wheeling on a large machine with tubes and one
large trap door. It looks something like a vacuum cleaner, with one large
tube leading off stage.*

Gadget Rocket Waste Disposal System.

Grime Minister Rocket Waste Disposal System.

Auntie Septic rushes forward to spray it, bowing to the royal family as she does so. Duster polishes it. Gadget prepares a largish sack of rubbish, placing in it the soot he has swept up

Princess Spotless Gosh. What does it do?

Gadget It gets rid of anything unwanted.

Duster (*to Princess Spotless; cheekily*) Would you like to go, your Highness?

Princess Spotless Ha ha funny ha ha. (*She kicks Duster*)

Duster instinctively raises his hand. Princess Spotless immediately starts crying.

Boo, hoo hoo hoo.

Queen Duster! Leave my little girl alone. (*To the Princess*) Come here, darling, Queenymummy look after babywaby. Nasty Duster won't hurt her.

King Hush, hush, my dear, please. (*He is most interested in the contraption*) How does it work, Gadget?

Gadget Simple, your Majesty.

Song 4—THE ROCKET SONG

Gadget   You stuff the rubbish in here
                                   Wait till you hear the system swallow it

(*He mimes the action*)

                                   Then shut the door and lock it
                                   The rubbish travels down this tube
                                   If you listen you can follow it

(*He mimes the listening*)

                                   Till it reaches the disposal rocket
                                   Ten, nine, eight, seven, six
                                   Five, four, three, two, one
                                   Lift off!

All applaud

King How exciting. Can I have a go?

Gadget Certainly, your Majesty. The machine is nearly full. One more sack of rubbish will set off the rocket ignition system.

King (*rising and gingerly picking up the sack*) Where do I throw it?

Gadget (*opening the trap door*) In here.

Queen Don't get your ermine grubby.

King No, dear.

Gadget pushes a switch. There is the noise of the engine running. The King throws in the sack. All wait a couple of seconds and watch. The King leans forward. The sack is suddenly thrown out of the door, knocking the King over. Gadget switches off

Gadget, how dare you. Is this a joke?

Gadget No, your Majesty. Please try again.

The Grime Minister helps the King up. Gadget switches on. The King picks up the sack and once more throws it in. As before, a pause. Then again the sack is thrown out. The King sees it in time and moves away: it knocks over Duster. Laughter. Gadget switches off.

Princess Spotless I think he's going to be a good Court Duster, Daddy. He makes *me* laugh.

Duster gets up angrily. Gadget busily and anxiously checks the machine.

Gadget Oh dear, oh dear, etc. Ah! I spot the error. I switched to blow instead of suck. Your Majesty, please, once more. (*He switches on*)

Song 4a—THE ROCKET SONG

King   You stuff the rubbish in here
                  Wait till you hear the system swallow it

There is the sound of a large swallow

                  Then shut the door and lock it
                  The rubbish travels down this tube
                  If you listen you can follow it

Noises of eating are heard

                  Till it reaches the disposal rocket
All   Ten, nine, eight, seven, six
                  Five, four, three, two one
                  Lift off!

At the end of the song, led by Gadget, all rush to the window. We hear a whirring sound and see, through the window, the rocket take off. "Ooohs" and "aaahs", and exclamations of "There it goes" come from everyone

During this Measle rushes on surreptitiously and picks up the telephone. His conversation may be obscured by the audience shouting out a warning, but we see from his reaction that all is well and he is instructed to carry on with the plot

Measle Hallo, Boss? M one-oh-one . . . In Palace . . . Message understood. Will proceed according to plan. Over and out.

Measle exits

The others return from the window, all effusive about Gadget's invention

King Congratulations, Gadget!
Queen A masterstroke!

Grime Minister No more rubbish in Hygenia!
Auntie Septic It's your best invention ever, Mr. Gadget.
Gadget Thank you, Auntie Septic.

In the middle of this excitement we hear the "bleep, bleep" we heard on the roof. All freeze

Grime Minister News flash.

All rush to television, which Gadget switches on

Television Voice . . . an enemy has been dropped over the Palace. He is described as of slight build, furry, and of a desperate character. He is armed, and though we have no news of his intentions in Hygenia, could well be dangerous.

There is a dramatic chord. Gadget switches off. A concerned hush

King Grime Minister, this could be serious.
Grime Minister Most serious, your Majesty.
King Has any subject seen anybody new or suspicious today?
Princess Spotless Only Duster.

All gasp and look at Duster

Auntie Septic But Duster's been working with me all day.
Duster Now look here, I don't know what you're getting at, but I don't like the sound of it . . .
Grime Minister Might I point out to your Majesties that Duster does not truly fit the description offered on the television—"of slight build" he may be, but "furry", I fancy not.
King True. Duster, we apologize.
Duster (*annoyed*) I should think so . . .

The others motion him to calm down

Thank you, your Majesty.
King Listen to me . . .
Grime Minister Hearken to his Majesty, King . . .
King All right, all right, skip that. This is an emergency. You are all to retire to your rooms early for the night. Whatever this furry invader is, we must protect ourselves against it.
Grime Minister Fear not, your Majesty. I will make instant moves to discover the intruder and expel him forthwith.
Princess Spotless Mummy, I'm frightened. Can Stainless come and keep me company tonight?
Queen Of course, my darling. Stainless, protect your young mistress.
King No, wait. He can't.
Princess Spotless Why not? It's not fair. (*She starts to blubber*)
King Stop blubbering. We must all keep calm. Stainless, my dear, must protect all of us.

Stainless looks terrified

"Of slight build" and "furry" sounds just about a cat's cup of tea. So he'll stay here and stand on guard. Come, my dear.

The Court exits to music, all except Stainless

No-one can help Stainless, who remains trembling

After a pause, Princess Spotless returns on tiptoe, having escaped for a moment

Princess Spotless taps Stainless on the shoulder, who jumps with terror. She calms him down

Princess Spotless It's only me. (*Whispering*) Come and see me later. The door will be open. Please.

Stainless nods

Princess Spotless dashes off

Tension music is heard as Stainless starts his guard duty. He walks one way, then the other, looking out for danger. When he reaches one side of the stage, he turns and walks towards the other

As Stainless does this, Measle follows him, walking warily backwards and therefore unaware of Stainless' presence

Suddenly Measle and Stainless both sense danger, and stop. By this time the audience will be shouting a warning. Gingerly, Stainless and Measle walk in a circle, round each other, still back to back. They then part, both walking forwards away from each other. They look, see nothing, then walk backwards towards each other. They cross each other, without touching, and turn slightly so that they are once again back to back, going round in a circle. All these movements are punctuated with tense sensings of danger. Now both relax, thinking they must have been mistaken. They back into each other. Both jump, then freeze

Then Measle runs round the room and exits the way the Court left, leaving Stainless petrified

The Lights fade to a Black-Out

SCENE 4

The Princess' bedroom

There are a bed, cupboard and window; and a telephone outside the door, on the corridor wall. Princess Spotless enters with Auntie Septic. The Princess wears a nightie

Princess Spotless But Auntie Septic, I don't *want* to go to bed. It's not fair.

Auntie Septic I'm sorry, your Majesty. Emergency. The King commands, we all obey. (*She sprays the bed*)

Princess Spotless Shan't.

Auntie Septic You must.

Princess Spotless Won't

Auntie Septic You will.

Princess Spotless Catch me, then.

Auntie Septic chases her round the bed good-humouredly. Princess Spotless enjoys this. She makes for the door

> *The Queen enters, carrying a bedtime drink, plus her own chocolates, which she eats through the scene. Princess Spotless bumps into her*

Queen (*with a roar*) BED!

Princess Spotless (*meekly as a lamb*) Yes, Mummy. (*She climbs into bed*)

Auntie Septic fetches a tray of cleansing cream, gargle, etc.

Queen Inspection.

Song 5—CLEAN ALL OVER

Queen and Auntie Septic
> Have you washed your hands?
> Have you cleaned your teeth?
> Have you rid your nails
> Of the dirt that's underneath?
> Have you brushed your hair?
> Have you scrubbed behind your ears?
> Are you clean all over now, Spotless dear?

Princess Spotless (*fed up*)
> Yes, I've washed my hands
> Yes, I've cleaned my teeth
> Yes, I've rid my nails
> Of the dirt that's underneath
> Yes, I've brushed my hair
> Yes, I've scrubbed behind my ears
> If I scrub much harder they'll disappear.

Queen and Auntie Septic (*acting out the words*)
> Rub in some cleansing cream
> Get off all the grime
> Now rub it off again

Princess Spotless   What a waste of time!

They sing the first and second verses as a round

Queen and Auntie Septic
> Aren't you glad you're clean all over?

Princess Spotless   I'm just glad—it's all over!

After the song, Auntie Septic picks up the tray

Auntie Septic Good night, sleep tight, your Majesty.
Princess Spotless Night, Auntie Septic.

Auntie Septic exits, leaving the door ajar

Mummy, will you read me a bedtime story?
Queen Sorry, Spotless, not tonight.
Princess Spotless But it's not fair. I *always* have a bedtime story.
Queen (*drawing the window curtains*) We don't *always* have enemies invading the Palace. So hurry up and down your bedtime drink and settle. Then I can turn the lights out.

As the Queen speaks, Measle enters the room furtively from the corridor

Unseen by the Queen, who has her back to him at the window, he deliberately takes a pill from a bottle and drops it into the bedtime drink. Audience reaction will try to warn the Queen and Princess Spotless, but they do not take any notice. The Queen turns round and, in the nick of time, Measle skedaddles under the bed. The Queen points sternly at the bedtime drink, and Princess Spotless, reluctantly, eventually drinks it. The Queen kisses her good night and takes the glass

The Queen exits, turning off the light as she goes

Pause. Princess Spotless starts snoring. Measle emerges in the gloom, gleefully checks that the bedtime drink has been drunk, then goes into the corridor. He checks that no-one is about, dials a telephone number, and waits. The following speech may be inaudible if the audience are still shouting a warning. In that case it should be mimed—"Mission successful"

Measle Hello, Boss? M. One-oh-one. Mission A accomplished. Over and out.

Measle exits.
   At the same moment the window curtains bulge as an intruder seems to be trying to get in. We then see it is Stainless

Stainless shakes the Princess gently to wake her. She turns over sleepily, to face him. He recoils in horror

Princess Spotless Hello, Stainless. Stainless, what is it?

Stainless turns on the lights and fetches a mirror. He hands it to Princess Spotless, who looks into it and screams loudly. We see that she has huge spots all over her face

Spots! I've got SPOTS! (*She screams again*)

The Lights fade to a Black-Out. The noisy ring of a telephone bell leads into the next scene

Scene 5

On the Palace roof

Weathervane has his back to us. Aerial is straining to hear the telephone conversation. In song, he relays the information to Weathervane

Song 6—THE PHONE MESSAGE

Aerial	They are phoning up the doctor
Weathervane	What for?
Aerial	Princess Spotless isn't well, and
	What's more—
	She's got spots upon her face—
	Poor Stainless—in disgrace!
	For he was meant to guard her door
Weathervane	What? Poor Stainless meant to guard her door
	What for?
Aerial	To protect her from that pest we saw.
Weathervane	Have they found the furry stranger?
Aerial	No news.
	They're still searching for the scoundrel
	No clues
	And the Queen is in a state
	The King says, at this rate
	Hygenia could be at war.
Weathervane	What? You mean an anti-germ-type war
	Once more?
Aerial	Yes, the war Hygenia won before.

Aerial My word, it's getting exciting. Better than the telly.

Weathervane Better indeed than *your* telly.

Aerial It's not *my* telly. I just help the programmes on their way down-stairs.

Weathervane They seem to have left their stamp on you.

Aerial What do you mean?

Weathervane You're almost as vulgar as they are.

Aerial Oh, shut up. (*With sudden vehemence*) And I'm fed up with rabbiting on to the back of your head.

Weathervane Can't help it. The wind commands and I obey. I'm stuck here till a suitable gust turns me. And I'm sorry if I was rude.

Aerial Oh, forget it. No wonder we're edgy, all this . . .

Aerial is interrupted by the "bleep, bleep" meaning "News Flash". He tunes himself in

Television Voice This is a news flash. A doctor is on his way to diagnose the Princess Spotless's mystery illness. She has been confined to her room. Meanwhile, the search goes on for the suspected intruder, believed to have something to do with the Princess's sudden attack. You are all asked to look out for a creature of slight build, furry, and of a desperate character.

Towards the end of the speech Measle himself climbs out of the chimney pot

The television voice continues under the dialogue

Anybody seeing him should not attempt to capture him: he could be very dangerous. In view of the seriousness of the situation, I will repeat the news flash. A doctor is on his way to diagnose, etc. (*He repeats as before*)
Weathervane (*seeing Measle*) Aerial, there he is. Hey you, whatever you are.
Aerial What do you think you're up to? They're all after you.
Weathervane Yes, your game will soon be up.

Measle takes no notice, but opens his case and tinkers inside

Aerial They're talking about you now.

Measle approaches Weathervane and stuffs a pill down his throat

Weathervane You'll never get away with it—you—how dare you . . . (*He gulps down the pill*)
Aerial You take your hands off him. Who are you, anyway?

Measle makes for Aerial with a phial of liquid

What are you doing? Leave my tubes alone . . .

Aerial is too late, Measle has poured the liquid in. Immediately the "news flash" sounds distorted, and finally fades out altogether

(*Weakly*) You'll pay for this.

Both Weathervane and Aerial are now whoozy, swaying a little on their moorings. Measle goes to the telephone wires, and fixes up his tapping equipment. He dials

Measle Hallo Boss? . . . Who's that? . . . I see. Message for him. Mission B accomplished.

A sudden gust of wind sends Weathervane round to face the audience. We see he is covered in spots

(*Into the telephone*) Signed M One-oh-one—Measle.

The music starts for the song. Measle quickly puts his gear away and then dramatically cuts the telephone wires

(*Cackling*) No more television, no more telephone.

Song 7—I'M A MEASLE

Measle

I'm a measle
Not a weasel or a mouse
But an evil cross between the two
And I warn you
With a measle in the house
There is precious little anyone can do.

I'm a measle
And I live up to my name
And my mission is to make you ill
No-one knows a
Way to stop my wicked game
When I strike and use my harmless-looking pill.

No-one can catch me—hee hee hee
But nothing can stop you catching me!

I'm a measle
An infectious little germ
Those I don't attack are rare and few
I'm so cunning
And as slippery as a worm
So watch out or you'll be struck with measles too
So watch out or I shall strike at all of you.

Cackling maniacally, Measle disappears down the chimney pot

Weathervane and Aerial are left powerless and ill, as—

the CURTAIN *falls*

ACT II

The Throne Room in the Palace

The Rocket Waste Disposal System is still there. The King and Queen are anxiously comforting Princess Spotless, who is being sprayed by Auntie Septic. The Grime Minister, Duster, Gadget and Stainless are also in attendance. The Queen is gorging chocolates as usual

Song 8—THE PRINCESS SPOTLESS IS SPOTTY

King, Queen, Grime Minister, Duster and Auntie Septic
> The Princess Spotless is spotty
> She is feeling pretty grotty
> The Princess Spotless is spotty
> From her brow to her botty
> She'd never got a spot before
> Now she's no space for one spot more.

> The Princess Spotless is spotty
> Since before she was a tot she
> From all spots has got off scot-free
> In her pram, on her potty
> She never bore the slightest trace
> But now she's got a spotty face

Queen
Princess Spotless
All
> Oh my poor spotty daughter
> Can I have a drink of water?
> She lies in bed
> Nearly dies in dread
> As she spies 'em spreading
> Like a rumour
> Is it any wonder that she's lost her sense of humour?

> The Princess Spotless is spotty
> And the problem posed is knotty
> The Princess Spotless is spotty
> From her brow to her botty
> She'd never got a spot before
> Now she's no space for one spot more.

After the song, the clock chimes from the Throne Room

Duster rushes out and returns with a tray of glasses

Grime Minister The Royal Gargle.

All do the gargling routine. Suddenly there is a loud knocking at the door

Duster, the door.

Duster goes to the door. In a moment he returns and whispers to the Grime Minister

Gadget stands by his machine. Stainless is trying to get nearer his mistress

Queen Stainless, stand aside. You're in disgrace.
King Fat lot of use you are, you cowardly cat.
Princess Spotless Don't bully him. He couldn't help it.
Queen No, and he *didn't* help, did he? Meant to be guarding us.
King Couldn't guard a tadpole.
Princess Spotless He raised the alarm.
Queen Only in fright.
Grime Minister (*announcing*) Doctor Spicknspan, your Majesties!

Doctor Spicknspan enters

Doctor Spicknspan Guten tag, bon jour, good day. Was ist de matter, as zey say, jawohl?
King How do you do, Doctor. Welcome. Long time no see.
Doctor Spicknspan Ja. Ist long time since.
King We have been so healthy.
Queen Till today. Our daughter has spots.
Doctor Spicknspan Spots? She is gespotty mit spotten? Ach so, how much?
King What?
Doctor Spicknspan How much?
King Oh, you mean how many? Spots? Oo, I suppose, seventeen, eighteen on her face, er . . .
Doctor Spicknspan No, no, no, no, no. How much will you pay me? Ha, ha, ha. You make me wealthy. I make her healthy. Ha, ha, ha, zat is my motto.
King Ha, ha, ha. (*Slightly nervous*) The price is immaterial.
Queen She is our daughter.
Doctor Spicknspan Very good. Bitte stand from ze patient.

All move. The Doctor sets to work. Music for tension. The Doctor takes the Princess's arm

Pulse. Say Ahh.

The Doctor places a thermometer in the Princess's mouth as she says "ahh". He nods in time with her pulse, which gets faster and faster. He stops, gets out a stethoscope, puts it on, and listens in. He apparently hears nothing, and looks worried

Princess Spotless (*with the thermometer still in her mouth*) Lower down.
Doctor Spicknspan What?
Princess Spotless My heart is lower down.
Doctor Spicknspan Ich cannot you hear. (*He points to the stethoscope in his ears*)
Princess Spotless (*taking out the thermometer, grabbing the end of the stethoscope and shouting down it*) My heart is lower down!

The Doctor jumps with the noise, takes the thermometer, looks at it and shakes his head

King Well?
Doctor Spicknspan She has—MEASLES.

There is a general gasp of horror

Song 9—IT'S THE FEVER!

Doctor Spicknspan   First you see the spots
Feel your temp'rature rise
Soon you're sticky and hot
With a pain behind the eyes
In three weeks it will be past
But it's nasty while it lasts
You must leave her—
It's the fever!

It's a bodily disorder
Of a minor common order
She is stricken
She is sick 'n
She's contagious
It's a typical distemper
So you mustn't lose your temper
It's not serious
King   She's delirious
It's outrageous!

All   First you see the spots
Feel your temp'rature rise
Soon you're sticky and hot
With a pain behind the eyes
In three weeks it will be past
But it's nasty while it lasts
We must leave here—
It's the fever!

Doctor Spicknspan   With a childish disposition
One is prone to this condition
She's infected
She's affected
By bacteria
It is true she is unhealthy
But your Majesty is wealthy
For a small fee
You can call me
And I'll clear her.

During the song, Measle enters unseen and pops a pill in the Queen's chocolate box. He exits unnoticed

All   First you see the spots
                                 Feel your temp'rature rise
                                 Soon you're sticky and hot
                                 With a pain behind the eyes
                                 In three weeks it will be past
                                 But it's nasty while it lasts
                                 We must leave her—
                                 It's the fever!

The song ends in gloom, and the music sombrely continues as the Doctor points to the Door

Doctor Spicknspan Ze Princess Spotless to her bed muss aller vite now.
Queen I'll take her. I'll just have my last choccy.

There is possible audience reaction to stop her taking the pill, but she pays no attention, scrumples the empty box and deliberately throws it into the Rocket Waste Disposal System

The Queen exits, taking Princess Spotless with her

Gadget checks that his machine is working all right—we hear the rocket noises

Gadget Psst. Your Majesty, the rocket.

                    Song 9a—THE ROCKET SONG (Reprise)
All   You stuff the rubbish in here
                                 Wait till you hear the system swallow it
                                 Then shut the door and lock it
                                 The rubbish travels down the tube
                                 If you listen you can follow it
                                 Till it reaches the disposal rocket
                                 Ten, nine, eight, seven, six,
                                 Five, four, three, two, one,
                                 Lift off!

Outside the window we see the rocket going off

Doctor Spicknspan May Ich interrupt zis mood of melancholia by collect-
    ing my fee?
King With pleasure. (*He waves to the Grime Minister to deal with it*)
Grime Minister Doctor Spicknspan, the bill.
Doctor Spicknspan Five hundred Hygenian pounds.
King What?
Doctor Spicknspan Please.
King Five hundred? Scandalous.
Doctor Spicknspan Do you want her to get better or not?
King But—five hundred?
Doctor Spicknspan Ich will much time have to spenden mit her. Leave it or
    take it.

King Very well

Screams are heard from off stage. All turn

The Queen enters. She is spotty

Queen Look at me! Look at me! Spots!

Auntie Septic rushes forward to give her a spray

Doctor Spicknspan Go away, go away. Your Majesty, kommen mit me, schnell schnell before it is too late.

Doctor Spicknspan hustles the Queen off

King Before it's too late? What's he talking about? Grime Minister!
Grime Minister Your Majesty?
King This measles must be catching.
Grime Minister Could lead to an epidemic, your Majesty. There has been so little illness in Hygenia, your subjects will not be strong enough to withstand it.
King An epidemic?
Grime Minister It could spread like wildfire.
King What are we to do? *I* could be next.
Gadget Your Majesty, might I suggest a television appearance? It would make me so proud if my television system could help in any . . .
King That's it. Speak to the Kingdom. Grime Minister, off you go. Tell our subjects to stay indoors. Measles must not take over Hygenia.
Grime Minister Maybe I should change my suit.
King Rubbish. This is an emergency.

The Grime Minister is pushed off

The others, hearing the King's last impassioned words, applaud his last line
(*Receiving the applause*) Thank you. (*He suddenly notices Duster standing there*) You, Duster. You've kept very quiet. I think you know more than meets the eye. I've never trusted you.
Duster But why not? I may be new, but I've done nothing—I haven't even told many jokes because of all this trouble. Why pick on me?
Auntie Septic (*calming him down*) Duster, that's enough. Your Majesty, I can vouch for Duster's true loyalty. You can be sure that both of us— and Gadget—will fight for Hygenia's safety—and your own.
Gadget Indeed, your Majesty, and this might perhaps be the moment to introduce my latest efforts towards the war against the unclean.
King Why certainly, Gadget.
Gadget The most up-to-date super-duper ultra-special make-your-eyes-pop-out-on-stalks—washing-machine.

Fanfare

Duster, Auntie Septic and Gadget go off and return leading on the machine

King Oh, how wonderful. A demonstration, please.
Duster Your Majesty, might I suggest—well, there is a danger—you see, your clothes may be infected.
King What? (*He immediately feels imaginary itches*)
Duster Infected with measles.
Auntie Septic Constant contact with the afflicted.
King Oooh. What can I do?
Gadget Wash them. In here. As part of the demonstration.
The King is unable to wait. Forgetting embarrassment, he starts to strip off
King Good idea. Infected? Ugh.

Music starts as the King gingerly removes his outer garments, revealing funny underwear. As each garment comes off it is passed at arm's length along the line, eventually reaching Gadget, who pops it in the machine. When all the clothes are in Gadget turns the knobs

Gadget Hot wash, spin dry, starch, disinfectant—here goes. (*He switches on*)

Noisy rhythmic mechanical sounds are heard, which help to accompany the song

Song 10—RUMBLE, RUMBLE

Gadget   Rumble, rumble
                                  Toss, turn, tumble
                                  The water churns round and about
                                  Rumble, rumble
                                  Toss, turn, tumble
                                  See the diff'rence as they all come out

The machine stops—maybe a green light comes on. Gadget steps forward and removes a garment. It is as stiff as a board

King Gadget, what have you done?
Auntie Septic Starch. Too much starch.
Gadget Apologies, apologies, your Majesty. Let's try again. (*Changing the switches accordingly and replacing the garment, Gadget turns the knobs on again*)

Song 10a—RUMBLE, RUMBLE (Reprise)

Gadget   Rumble, rumble
                                  Toss, turn, tumble
                                  The water churns round and about
                                  Rumble, rumble
                                  Toss, turn, tumble
                                  See the diff'rence as they all come out

The machine stops. Gadget removes a garment, and another, and another—all are tiny

Duster Oh no, they've shrunk!

King Gadget, you bodger! They're ruined.

Gadget Apologies, apologies, your Majesty. (*He starts to push the machine off*) I'll take it back to the workshop. Oh dear, oh dear, oh dear . . .

Gadget exits with the machine, terrified

King And next time, test it with your own garments, and not the Royal Outfit number three. Hey, wait! Return! Turn on the telly. I want to view the Grime Minister's speech to the Kingdom

Gadget sheepishly returns, switches on the television, then exits

Fanfare from the television, Duster and Auntie Septic stand to attention. The set then runs down with an awful sound. Then—nothing. Duster and Auntie Septic relax from the "at attention" pose they adopted when the fanfare started

Don't say *that's* not working either. (*He bashes the set*)

Duster Can I help, your Majesty? (*He bashes the set too*)

King Can't understand it. All these spots all over the screen.

Dramatic chord. Realization registers

Spots!

Auntie Septic Measles!

Duster But that's impossible. Whoever heard of a measly telly?

King (*transfixed*) Stop talking. Telephone Gadget.

Duster goes to the telephone and dials. Dramatic chord

Duster The line's dead. It's out of order.

King What's going on? Hygenia is being slowly paralysed.

Auntie Septic I'll go and find Gadget, your Majesty.

King Thank you, Auntie Septic. Tell him it's an emergency. He's to go up on the roof and investigate the ailing telly and the failing phone.

Auntie Septic Straightaway, your Majesty.

Auntie Septic exits

The King realizes he is alone with Duster for the first time. He eyes him suspiciously

Duster Don't get in a paddy, your Majesty. I'll make you laugh.

King I don't feel like laughing.

Duster Listen to this. What's green and hairy and goes up and down?

King I don't know. What *is* green and hairy and goes up and down?

Duster A gooseberry in a lift. (*He roars with laughter*)

There is no reaction from the King

King Was it on a saucer?

Duster What?

King This gooseberry. Was it on a saucer?
Duster I don't know.
King Well, what a stupid joke. Most unhygienic—a gooseberry in contact
  with the floor of a lift. Ugh. Was it a washed gooseberry?
Duster I don't know. I didn't think it mattered.
King Didn't think it mattered? Of course it matters. Unwashed goose-
  berries give you collywobbles. It sounds a most unhygienic joke. Make
  the next one cleaner. Remember where you are.
Duster Yes, your Majesty.
King (*muttering to himself*) Unwashed gooseberries on lift floors. Disgusting!
Duster Sorry, your Majesty.
King Fetch my dressing-gown. It's so embarrassing, wandering around in
  one's underwear, even if it is in one's own palace.
Duster One dressing-gown coming up, your Majesty.

Duster exits

King He seems harmless enough. I must have been wrong about him.

From off stage there is a muffled scream and a thud

  Ah, Gadget's on his way. Hope he's all right on that ladder.

*Measle enters disguised as Duster—in fact wearing Duster's outer gar-
ments. He carries the King's dressing-gown. It will be most effective if
even the audience do not realize for a while what has happened*

Measle (*imitating Duster*) Dressing-gown, your Majesty.

The King puts on his dressing-gown, helped by Measle

King Ah, thank you, Duster. I was just saying to myself, I hope Gadget
  will be safe on the roof.
Measle I'm sure he can take care of himself, your Majesty.
King Let's hope we can *all* take care of ourselves, eh? Don't want a spotty
  Court. I say, how do you think measles comes?
Measle You catch them.
King Yes, but how do they start? How do they come in the first place?
Measle Well, your Majesty, perhaps there is a creature called Measle,
  who brings it by air—sort of slight, furry creature of a desperate character.
King (*roaring with laughter*) Ha, ha! Now that *is* a good joke, Duster.
  You're improving. Creatures called Measles. Ha ha!

*Measle swiftly pops a pill in the King's open mouth. The King gulps and
swallows it*

Measle No, not creatures called Measles. (*Throwing off his disguise*) A
  creature called Measle—ME!

The King screams with horror

King The pill, the pill?

Measle My signature, of course. You'll see spots soon!

Duster, in his underwear, reels in, recovering from being knocked out by Measle

Measle sees Duster and starts to run off. Duster blocks his path. The King gets up to help. They chase one another round

Eventually Measle escapes through the window

The King and Duster are left bumping into each other, as the Lights fade to a Black-Out

SCENE 2

On the Palace Roof

There is the loud noise of a heavy wind. During the scene sudden gusts make Weathervane revolve

Song 10b—IT'S THE FEVER!

Weathervane and Aerial

	First you see the spots
	Feel your temp'rature rise
	Soon you're sticky and hot
	With a pain behind the eyes
Weathervane	In three weeks it will be past
	But it's nasty while it lasts
Aerial	I believe ya
Both	It's the fever!

We see, from behind, a ladder raised against the roof. Gadget appears and sets to work on the telephone wires

Gadget Have you two caught it as well?

Aerial What does it look like, cock? Ooh, I feel terrible, all weak about the tubes

Weathervane Have they apprehended the monstrous Measle yet?

A gust of wind sends Weathervane hurtling round. He groans

Gadget Not yet. (*Having finished mending the wires, he produces a device with headphones and a dial, and sets it up, attaching it to the wires*)

Aerial If I hadn't been screwed to this wretched roof, I'd have given him what for. (*Speaking so vehemently makes him giddy, and he groans*)

Gadget I'll see what I can do for you in a tick. (*He dials a number*) Though I reckon it's not technical, more medical. Fancy some oil?

Aerial groans

Cod liver, castor or sewing machine, I wonder which would be best. (*A voice answers the phone*) Hallo. Your Majesty?

A light comes on in the corridor outside the Princess's bedroom. The King is on the telephone, spotty

King Yes?
Gadget (*articulating well*) Can you hear me?
King Don't shout. My head's aching like a tom-tom as it is.
Gadget What's the matter?
King The matter? Measles is the matter.
Gadget You, too?
King Yes. The Doctor's with me now. What did you want?
Gadget You told me to mend the phone.
King Then mend it.
Gadget I have, your Majesty, you're speaking into it now.
King Oh, of course. Well mended, Gadget.
Gadget Thank you, your Majesty.

They both go to ring off

Oh, before you go . . .
King What is it now?
Gadget Weathervane and Aerial are very poorly—they've caught measles too. Could you send the Doctor up to see them?
King Very well; though it's all getting far too expensive. But I must see the Grime Minister on the telly. (*He rings off*)

The light on the corridor fades. A sudden "bleep-bleep" sends Gadget over to Aerial

Television Voice This is a news flash. Here is the Grime Minister, to speak to the Kingdom . . .

But almost as soon as it starts, the voice is distorted, and finally peters out. Gadget fiddles with knobs and tubes, but it is no good

Aerial I can't—I can't hold on to it—I try to force it downstairs—but . . .
Gadget Don't waste your energy. The Doctor's coming in a tick.

A sudden gust is too much for Weathervane. As though seasick, he collapses in a heap, groaning; still, of course, "anchored" to the roof. Gadget rushes over to him

Doctor Spicknspan arrives, carrying a large hypodermic syringe. He goes to Aerial

There you are. These two are in pretty bad shape.
Doctor Spicknspan Mmm. (*He examines Aerial, feels the pulse of a tube, etc.*) Yes, it's measles. Ich will care of them take.
Gadget Good. I'll be off, then. Good luck, you two. Soon be better. (*Descending the ladder*) Just a spot of bother—well, several spots of bother, really . . .

Gadget disappears

Doctor Spicknspan (*raising his hypodermic syringe*) Close your eyes. Zis
will make you sleepen sound, jawohl?
Aerial But I can't go to sleep. I've got to be awake for news flashes—I . . .

*Too late—the Doctor has injected him. He looks stunned, then becomes
paralysed stiff, snoring mechanically. The Doctor crosses to Weathervane
and examines him*

Doctor Spicknspan Asleepen sound already. Zat is good. (*He rushes to the
telephone connections*)

*Music for tension. The Doctor produces a tapping device like the one Measle
used before. He attaches it, and dials. We hear a faint ringing tone*

(*Impatiently*) Hurryupensie, hurryupensie.

*Unseen by the Doctor, Weathervane wakes up and overhears the following.
If even the Doctor's gaze comes round to him he pretends to be asleep*

Hallo . . . Headquarters? . . . Listensie carefully. Message to Reinforcement Officer. Measle overworked and vulnerable. Send Measlygerm
Unit Two immediately. Immediately. Over and out. (*He produces a pair
of scissors and cuts through the telephone wires. Laughing, he climbs
down the ladder, forgetting his tapping equipment, and leaving Weathervane very much awake and horrified*)

Music begins as the Lights fade to a Black-Out

Scene 3

The Princess's Bedroom

*The King, Queen and Princess Spotless, all in nightgowns, sit spottily in or
on the bed. Stainless is forlornly lying at their feet*

Song 10c—THE PRINCESS SPOTLESS IS SPOTTY (Reprise)

King	It's true the Queen can be dotty
	But I've never seen her spotty
Queen	And though the King can be potty
	I have not seen him spotty
Both	Since Hygenia received her name
	Since Hygenia achieved her fame.

King, Queen and Princess Spotless

The Royal Family is spotty
It is feeling pretty grotty
The Royal Family is spotty
From its brow to its botty
It seldom got a spot before
Now there's no space for one spot more.

King Why isn't Stainless spotty?

Queen He must be immune, dear. Stainless steel must be difficult for the Measle to penetrate.

King Useless animal. Should be out there, tracking the monster down.

Stainless looks terrified

Princess Spotless Daddy, don't be horrid. It's not fair. Stainless isn't used to jobs like that.

King He doesn't seem to be used to any job. Lazy perishing pet.

Princess Spotless (*comfortably*) Don't listen, Stainless.

King Well, it's true. I can remember the days when a cat was a cat. Fought vermin every day before breakfast—*for* breakfast, in fact.

Queen But my dear, you must remember, Stainless has never *seen* vermin till now. It's the price we have to pay for hygiene.

Princess Spotless Yes, you can't expect him to fight.

Queen He has no instinct for it.

King Rubbish, he's a coward. All the faculties for sniffing out the enemy but doesn't use them. A coward. And as a result we're stuck here spotty with the prospect of an epidemic. Hygenia's not used to such a thing. It won't be strong enough to withstand it.

The Grime Minister enters the corridor. He knocks, but does not enter the infected area, shouting through the door

Yes?

Grime Minister Your Majesties, I'm returned from my television fiasco. I failed.

King We know.

Queen You didn't fail, Grime Minister, you did your best.

King Unlike Stainless.

Princess Spotless Daddy, please.

King Listen, Grime Minister. Don't let it spread. Keep my subjects indoors, spread the word.

Queen Get Gadget to invent something.

King But whatever you do, *catch that measle!*

The Grime Minister turns to go. We see his face for the first time. It is covered in spots. Dramatic chord. The audience in all probability tell him, but in any case he touches his face, and realizes.

Grime Minister I think I have already, your Majesty. (*He enters the bedroom and forlornly sits on the bed with the others*)

Song 10d—THE PRINCESS SPOTLESS IS SPOTTY (Reprise)

Grime Minister   I hate to state that I'm spotty
                        It's a statement that is grotty
                        And yet it's true I am spotty
                        From my brow to my botty

Now this Minister of State must state
I think I am about to faint . . .

The Grime Minister faints into the arms of the King. All freeze as the Lights cross-fade to the Palace roof, where Weathervane is leaning across still anchored by his base, to attempt to wake Aerial

Weathervane (*struggling*) Please, old friend, wake up. The phone! It's a matter of life and death. (*Attempting an army-type voice*) Wakey, wakey, rise and shine!

No reaction

Oh well, nothing for it. I must try to remember what Gadget did.

Music for tension. Weathervane stretches bravely to his full length and makes his way with an effort to the telephone wires. He can just reach them. With a great effort he manages to join them again

Done it! (*He picks up the Doctor's tapping device which he left in error, attaches it, and dials a number*)

The Lights come up on the Princess's bedroom as the phone rings on the wall of the corridor outside. The Royal Family and the Grime Minister react to it

At the same moment Doctor Spicknspan enters the corridor with his large syringe. He stops, amazed

Doctor Spicknspan But I gesnapped ze wires. (*He nervously approaches the phone, then picks up the receiver*) Hallo? M One-oh-one? Head-quarters? Who is zis?

Stainless jumps up, having recognized the code name. He listens at the door. Meanwhile, on the roof, Weathervane is shocked

Weathervane M One-oh-one? (*To himself*) Measle!

Stainless quickly beckons all the Royal Family to the door and mimes excitedly something about "roof", "evil monster", etc., meaning that he recognizes the code name from when he was on the roof as Measle arrived

Doctor Spicknspan Vat do you vant, M One-oh-one? Ich busy am.
Weathervane Er—nothing, nothing. (*Imitating Measle*) Mission proceeding —er message stood under—er—understood—over and out. (*In a panic, he tears the telephone wires apart. Wiping his forehead, he starts putting them together again*)

The Lights on the roof fade to Black-Out

Doctor Spicknspan Hallo, hallo, come backnsie. Are you all right? Measle. *Measle!*

Big chord. Big reaction among the Royal Party

Oh, stupid phone.

Doctor Spicknspan slams down the receiver, making the Royal Family hop back to bed. The Grime Minister hides behind the door. Doctor Spicknspan picks up his hypodermic syringe, knocks and enters the bedroom

Your Majesties, guten tag, bon jour, good day. Injection time, if you please, jawohl?

As the Doctor walks into the room, the Royal Family shrink back in fear

Do not vorry viz ze hypodermic. It will do you good.

The King is nearly speechless

King N-n-n-now l-l-listen to m-me, Sp-Sp-Span'nspick . . .
Queen Don't come near us.
Doctor Spicknspan Guten himmel. Vat are you speaking about?

Princess Spotless stands

Princess Spotless It's you, isn't it? You're behind it all! Measles. You've given us measles. Hygenia—the cleanest Kingdom in the world, and you've given us disease, putting fear and misery into the lives of every human being——

Stainless nudges her

—and cat.
Doctor Spicknspan (*listening with rising fury*) Ja, ja, ja, You are right. (*Manically*) I am ze Boss. But vat do you expect?

Song 11—REJECTED!

Doctor Spicknspan Hygenia for years and years perfect health has enjoyed
And all that time—I've been unemployed.

I've no money
It's not funny
I am starving in my attic
With nothing to do
'Cos no-one's ill
Or needs my skill
I'm automatic-
'lly rejected by you.

Fuddy duddies
Scorned my studies
Said disease I'd never banish
They called me a quack
And my success
Meant even less—
I made it vanish
I can make it come back.

I made you healthy
Opened the door

To a life free of strife and pain
Did you make me wealthy?
No, you made me poor
Now I'll make you suffer again.
I'll have money
It's so funny
I won't starve up in my attic
With nothing to do
'Cos now you're ill
You need my skill
I'm automatic-
'lly accepted—no long-
-er I'm rejected—stand back
You'll be injected
If you try to attack
No longer I'm rejected
By you.

At the end of the song, threatening the others with the hypodermic, he stands quivering, unaware of the Grime Minister's presence behind the door. The Grime Minister creeps up on him

Doctor Spicknspan So, don't anybody try to stoppen me. If you think you can beat me, you are wrong, wrong, wrong.

The Grime Minister grabs Doctor Spicknspan, but soon lets go when the hypodermic is pointed at him—he joins the others by the bed

You see. It is foolish to standen in my way. You vill never escape my clutches, never.

Doctor Spicknspan exits, locking the door

Grime Minister Locked!

The Lights cross-fade to the Palace roof. Weathervane is still trying to put the telephone wires together again

Weathervane Oh—fiddle! It's so fiddly. (*He finishes the job*) Done it! (*He attaches the device again and dials the number*)

The Lights come up on the corridor only

SCENE 4

Outside the Princess's bedroom

It is important to isolate this area, or the audience will yell warnings to the Royal Party, in the bedroom. The phone rings. Duster, in his underwear, enters. Just as he goes to answer the phone he sees Measle, disguised as Duster, approaching. He thinks quickly, and decides to hide. He gets out of sight as Measle reaches the phone and picks up the receiver

Measle (*still imitating Duster*) Hallo, hallo, Duster speaking.
Weathervane Thank goodness. Now, listen very carefully. Weathervane here.

Song 11a—THE PHONE MESSAGE (Reprise)

Weathervane	Take a message to the King and Be quick
Measle	Take a message to the King? But He's sick
Weathervane	Say he's got no time to waste A battle must be faced For the Measlygerms are on their way—
Measle	What! The Measlygerms are on their way?
Weathervane	Today!
Both	For the Measlygerms are on their way

Throughout the song, Duster listens to Measle. He reacts horrified

Weathervane So don't forget. Inform his Majesty.
Measle Certainly, certainly. His Majesty will be informed. Cheerio. (*He replaces the receiver*) His Majesty will *not* be informed.

Measle exits laughing

Duster (*emerging*) His Majesty *will* be informed. (*He knocks on the bedroom door*)

The Lights come up inside the bedroom. The Royal Party, plus the Grime Minister, are all feeling ill. Stainless alone is able to wander round from one to the other

Grime Minister (*weakly*) Who's there?
Duster It's me, Duster.
King Are you spotty yet?
Duster No. As spotless as Princess Spotless was before she got spotty, if you see what I mean.
Queen What do you want?
Duster I've just heard from Weathervane. Reinforcement Measlygerms are on their way. A right royal battle's on the cards.
Grime Minister Listen, Duster. We are all too ill to cope. Can you lead the defence?
Duster I'll have a go, Grime Minister.
King This is your chance to prove your loyalty to royalty.
Queen The future of Hygenia is in your hands.
Duster Righto.
Grime Minister Ask Auntie Septic to give you a hand.

Duster Leave it to me. Duster is going to have a dust-up!
All Good luck, be careful, etc.

Duster exits

Princess Spotless Do you think he'll be all right?
Grime Minister I've always believed in him, your Majesty.
Princess Spotless I wish Stainless would be brave.
King You're wasting your breath. Cowardly cat.

Song 12—YOU COULD BE A HERO

Princess Spotless   *(to Stainless)*
                          You could be a hero
                          If you tried
                          To face the danger
                          Instead of hiding
                          It wouldn't take long
                          To prove that your courage isn't zero
                          Yes, you could be a hero
                          And prove ev'rybody wrong

                          You could be a hero
                          If you'd fight
                          To save Hygenia
                          And don't be frightened
                          It wouldn't take long
                          To prove that your courage isn't zero
                          Yes, you could be a hero
                          And prove that you're really strong.

The Lights fade to a Black-Out

SCENE 5

The Throne Room in the Palace

*The Rocket Waste Disposal System and the Washing Machine are still there.
Duster enters with Auntie Septic*

Auntie Septic But how many Measlygerms did he say?
Duster He didn't. Just "reinforcements". But I reckon there'll be enough
to cause an epidemic.
Auntie Septic We must stop them.
Duster Exactly. (*Taking in the audience*) Every citizen is at risk. Everybody
must protect themselves against a Measlygerm attack.

*The audience should be encouraged to think of ideas. The following dialogue
should be taken as a guide*

How do you get rid of germs?

Auntie Septic I spray them.

Duster Yes, but *we* can't. How can we protect ourselves against germs if we can't spray them?

Auntie Septic A mask. Like they wear in hospitals.

Duster Good idea. Where do we find masks for everybody?

Auntie Septic Anything will do. A handkerchief. The edge of a pullover . . .

Duster (*to the audience*) All right, citizens—everybody find a mask. Stop the germs getting in.

If necessary, Auntie Septic and Duster go into the audience to give help. When this is accomplished the dialogue continues

I've got another idea. Any sign of danger, we should all hold our noses. Stop the germs running up them. Let's all try that.

All are encouraged to hold their noses

Fine. So when you hear the words "Masks" or "Noses", you know what to do.

Auntie Septic I say! I've just thought of something.

Duster Yes?

Auntie Septic A trick. If the Measlygerms thought we weren't worth attacking, they'd leave us alone.

Duster What'd make them think that?

Auntie Septic If we all had—*measles!*

Duster Yes! Spots. We must all have big spots.

Auntie Septic And pretend we're ill and powerless.

Duster Good. Now—(*to the audience*)—what have you got for spots— something to hold against your face? Coins? Good idea. Pieces of paper? Yes—tear a few spot shapes. Auntie Septic and I will help you.

Gadget enters

Gadget Can I help too?

Duster Of course, Gadget. And then you can stand by with the Washing Machine and the Rocket Waste Disposal System in case they come in useful.

Duster, Gadget and Auntie Septic all help the audience to get spotty. (It may be possible to have, as a publicity gimmick, self-adhesive spots attached to a free programme, or under the seats)

(*When all are ready*) Now don't forget, everyone. If you see a Measly- germ, pretend to be very ill—a little green, perhaps—plus the spots. Only in emergency, if we shout the instructions "Masks" and "Noses", will it mean the trick has failed.

The clock chimes

Oo! The Royal Gargle! That'd be a good start. Everybody, the Royal Gargle!

The audience is encouraged to mime taking a draught, gargling and drinking

Gadget Terrific!

Voices are heard off

Doctor Spicknspan (*off*) Zis vay.

The Measlygerms are heard noisily approaching

Duster This is it!
Auntie Septic Good luck, everybody!

Duster, Auntie Septic and Gadget hide

Doctor Spicknspan enters with the Measlygerms. The Doctor brandishes his hypodermic

Doctor Spicknspan Now, spread out. And forgetten-sie not. No-one to be spared is. Every citizen must be spotty.

Music as the battle commences

All exit except Measlygerm One

Measlygerm One looks about him, sees the audience, registers delight and, advances. If necessary, Duster, Gadget and Auntie Septic emerge to encourage groaning and "ill"-acting

Measlygerm One Aha! (*He notices*) Oh. You're all spotty already.

Measlygerm turns, and sees Duster peering round to see how the audience are doing. A fight ensues, like a bullfight, Duster using his duster as a cape. Measlygerm One is deceived and falls over a couple of times, but then Duster is overwhelmed and forced to the ground. Measlygerm One tries to make him swallow a pill. At this moment Auntie Septic runs on and sprays Measlygerm One, making him leave Duster and reel towards the Rocket Waste Disposal System. Gadget emerges and eagerly, though in a panic, turns switches. Auntie Septic sprays Measlygerm One into the "vacuum", but he shoots out again, knocking over Duster who has just got up. Consternation, because Gadget has turned the wrong switch

Auntie Septic's attention is distracted by the arrival of Measlygerm Two, if possible through the audience, checking that each person is spotty

Measlygerm Two reaches the stage and is rounded up, with Measlygerm One, by Auntie Septic, who sprays them vehemently

Duster Ready, Gadget (*To the audience*) Can you help? Blow, please, as hard as you can.

The audience help to blow the two Measlygerms towards the "vacuum". Measlygerm One is sucked up and vanishes, Gadget having turned the correct switch, but Measlygerm Two escapes and runs off. There is a brief pause for self-congratulation

Measlygerm Three enters

All on stage hide. Measlygerm Three sees the audience. Again they react "ill"

Measlygerm Three Aha! (*Noticing*) My, what a spotty lot.

Measlygerm Three turns back and sees Gadget. He chases him round the room until Gadget runs behind the Washing Machine and quickly opens the lid. Measlygerm Three runs up and falls inside. Gadget shuts the lid and switches on. The indicator turns to "On", on "Starch". The audience is encouraged to sing with Gadget, as well as Auntie Septic and Duster, who return from hiding

Song 12a—RUMBLE, RUMBLE (Reprise)

Gadget, Duster and Auntie Septic
> Rumble, rumble
> Toss, turn, tumble
> The water churns round and about
> Rumble, rumble
> Toss, turn, tumble
> See the diff'rence as they all come out.

As the song ends, Gadget switches off and opens the door of the machine. A dazed, stiff, starched Measlygerm Three hobbles out towards the Rocket Waste Disposal System. Auntie Septic sprays him. The audience is encouraged to blow again. Measlygerm Three is sucked up. All on stage hide again

Measlygerm Two enters. He is sniffing, trying to follow a scent

Measlygerm Two (*calling*) Measlygerm Three-ee. Where are you? (*Seeing the audience*) You didn't see where he went, did you?
Duster emerges and encourages the audience to direct Measlygerm Two to the Washing Machine. Auntie Septic sprays him en route. He follows the advice of the audience, and Gadget and Duster speedily tip him in. Gadget turns the indicator from "Starch" and switches on. Again the audience is encouraged to join in

Song 12b—RUMBLE, RUMBLE (Reprise)

Gadget, Duster and Auntie Septic
> Rumble, rumble
> Toss, turn, tumble
> The water churns round and about
> Rumble, rumble
> Toss, turn, tumble
> See the diff'rence as they all come out.

As the song ends, Gadget switches off and opens the door of the machine, and a shrunk, dazed mini-Measlygerm—perhaps played by a child—totters out and, blown by the audience and sprayed by Auntie Septic, is sucked up into the Rocket Waste Disposal System. There is another pause for self-congratulation, then Duster points off, and all, terrified, hide again

Measle enters, still wearing Duster's clothes

Measle (*to the audience*) You potty lot of spotty clots. Do you think you fool me? Measle? M One-oh-one? Well, you don't. It's about time somebody taught you not to play tricks on nice friendly Measlygerms. So, I'm coming to give you all a taste of *real* measles. (*He advances into the auditorium*)

Duster and Auntie Septic rush out and shout "Masks" and "Noses". Measle hears them and a chase ensues around the auditorium, all the time the audience being encouraged to protect themselves by the "Masks" and "Noses" method. They all reach the stage again

Stainless the cat enters at the same moment

Duster, Auntie Septic and Gadget stand aside as Stainless tackles Measle single-handed. The two creatures fight, the advantage veering from one to the other. Finally Stainless wins, or, at least, holds Measle down strongly enough for Duster to dash out and find Measle's pills, and to force one down his throat. Auntie Septic sprays the while

Duster There! A taste of your own medicine!
Measle No! Help! I don't want to get measles, etc., etc.

Measle is pushed and blown by the audience, protesting, into the Rocket Waste Disposal System. A sound tells us it is now full

Gadget It's full!

The audience is encouraged to join in the song, particularly the count-down

Song 12c—THE ROCKET SONG (Reprise)

Gadget, Duster and Auntie Septic
>You stuff the rubbish in here
>Wait till you hear the system swallow it
>Then shut the door and lock it
>The rubbish travels down this tube
>If you listen you can follow it
>Till it reaches the disposal rocket
>Ten, nine, eight, seven, six,
>Five, four, three, two, one,
>Lift off!

As the song ends we see the rocket taking off outside the window. Stainless, Duster, Auntie Septic and Gadget wave it good-bye

A furious Doctor Spicknspan enters, brandishing his hypodermic

Doctor Spicknspan (*to all, including the audience*) You stupid meddlers. You zinken sie victorious are. But wiz one jab of zis you go to sleep. Wiz *two* jabs you never wake up.

Doctor Spicknspan advances towards the others, who back away slowly. Then suddenly Duster starts running. The others follow. A chase ensues across the front of the stage

1. *Duster is followed by Auntie Septic, Gadget and Stainless, all chased off R by Doctor Spicknspan*

2. *Stainless enters R, followed by Gadget, Auntie Septic and Duster, chased by Doctor Spicknspan. Stainless breaks off and hides. All the others exit L. Stainless thinks—wanting help against the Doctor—and then quickly exits R*

3. *Doctor Spicknspan enters L, chased by Auntie Septic ferociously spraying, and then by Duster and Gadget. Gadget is panting heavily, and is left behind on stage to catch his breath*

4. *Duster enters R, chased inadvertently by Auntie Septic, followed by Doctor Spicknspan. Duster and Auntie Septic exit L. Gadget manages to trip up Doctor Spicknspan. The hypodermic syringe falls from his hands and Gadget swiftly picks it up and brandishes it dangerously towards the Doctor, who gets up and flees off L, followed by Gadget*

5. *Stainless enters R, leading on the Grime Minister, the King, the Queen and Princess Spotless. All wear masks and hold their noses. All exit L*

6. *Princess Spotless enters L, followed by the Queen, King and Grime Minister, chased by a manic Gadget wielding his hypodermic syringe. All exit R.*

7. *Doctor Spicknspan enters L, looks tentatively about, and decides to escape through the window. He starts to climb*

8. *Duster and Auntie Septic enter L, searching. The audience shouts out that the Doctor is there. When Duster and Auntie Septic see him, they rush to the window and pull the Doctor away from it*

9. *Gadget enters R, exhausted, followed by the King, the Queen, Princess Spotless and the Grime Minister. As the Doctor is pulled backwards by Duster and Auntie Septic, he backs into the hypodermic held by Gadget, and immediately crumples asleep. Auntie Septic gives him a spray and then, exhausted, falls behind him*

King Congratulations to you all.

Queen Have a chocolate each. You deserve it.

Duster (*to all, including the audience*) Safe to remove your masks now, and if you're still holding your noses—let noses goeses!

King As for you, Duster, never shall I doubt you again. And thank you, too, Gadget.

Princess Spotless What about Stainless, Daddy?

Duster He finished off Measle, your Majesty.

King As I always said, the bravest cat in the Kingdom.

Grime Minister What shall I do with the Doctor, your Majesty?

Duster I'd give him the second jab. (*To the audience*) Wouldn't you?

King (*calming the audience*) I think we should lock him up. After all, he's
our only doctor, and we may need him.

Princess Spotless Maybe you'd better pay him, even when he doesn't
have to work, Daddy.

Duster and Gadget pick up Doctor Spicknspan

King Good idea; save any more trouble like this! Take him away.

*Gadget and Duster walk away with Doctor Spicknspan. As they do so,
Auntie Septic is revealed motionless behind him. All stop*

Princess Spotless Auntie. (*She runs to her and tries to wake her. No good*)
She's empty. She used up all her spray trying to save us.

Queen We owe her a great deal.

King Thank you, Auntie.

Silence. Then the Grime Minister and Stainless lift her

Both "bodies" are carried off, to music

There is a sudden "bleep, bleep", which changes the mood

A news flash! A news flash!

Princess Spotless turns on the television

Queen Aerial must be better.

King We're all better now!

Princess Spotless Shhh, Daddy, Listen.

*Duster, Gadget, Stainless and the Grime Minister rush back to see the
news flash*

Television Voice This is a news flash. The invasion of Hygenia by measles
is over. After a struggle in the Palace, thanks to the bravery of several
members of the palace staff, all danger of a measles epidemic has been
defeated. Hygenia can breathe freely once more.

*Princess Spotless turns off the television. All cheer. The Lights come up on
the roof. Aerial and Weathervane, both recovered, join in the final chorus*

	Song 12d—HYGENIA (Reprise)
All	A kingdom of worth
	Hygenia
	A kingdom of mirth
	Hygenia

Of dirt there's a dearth
It's the cleanest kingdom on earth
The kingdom of our birth
Hygenia.

CURTAIN

FURNITURE AND PROPERTY LIST

SUGGESTED GROUND PLANS

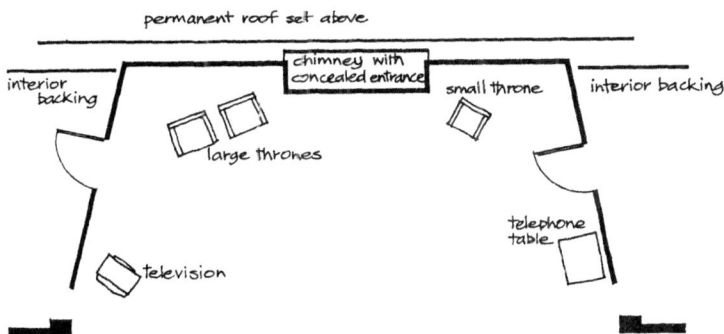

permanent roof set above

chimney with
concealed entrance

interior backing

small throne

interior backing

large thrones

telephone table

television

ACT I Sc 3
ACT II Scs 1 & 5

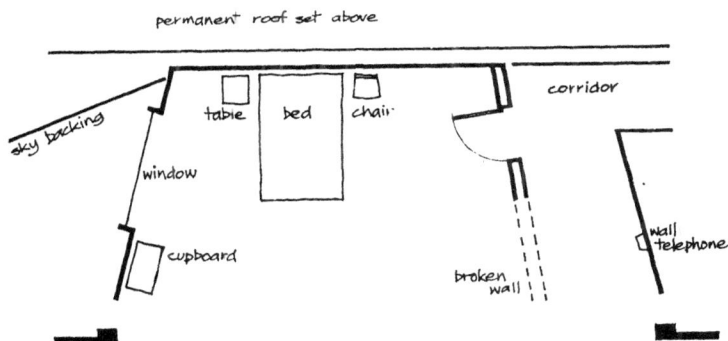

permanent roof set above

corridor

sky backing

table   bed   chair

window

wall telephone

cupboard

broken wall

ACT I Sc 4
ACT II Sc 2

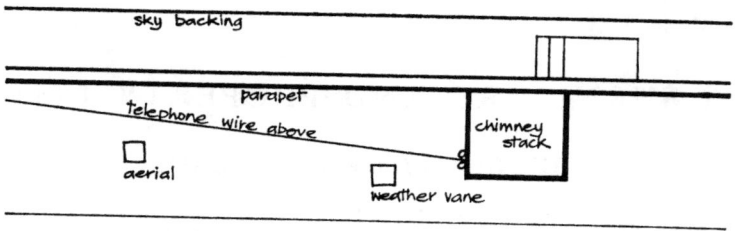

ACT I Scs 2 & 5
ACT II Sc 2

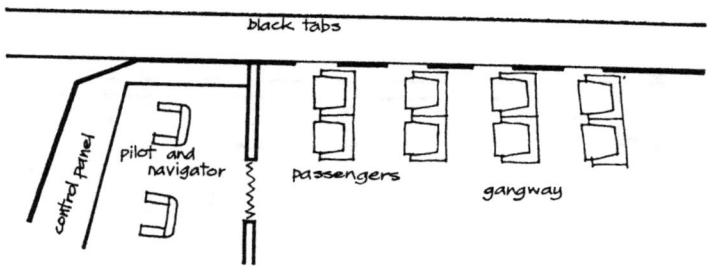

ACT I Sc 1

ACT I

SCENE 1

On stage: Aeroplane control panel with microphone and fittings
Seats for pilot, navigator and passengers
Tray of drinks for Stewardess

SCENE 2

Parapet
Chimney stack and telephone wires
Loudspeaker concealed near Aerial for TV voices

SCENE 3

2 large thrones
1 smaller throne
Television set
Table. *On it:* clock, telephone
Above fireplace, inside: bag of soot

SCENE 4

Bed and bedding
Cupboard
Bed table. *On it:* mirror
Small chair
Window curtains
In corridor: wall telephone

SCENE 5

As Scene 2

Off stage: Gun (**Measle**)
Parachute (**Measle**)
Small suitcase. *In it:* wire cutters and other tools, headphones, dialling apparatus (**Measle**)
Duster (**Duster**)
Spraying apparatus (**Auntie Septic**)
Box of chocolates (**Grime Minister**)
Lollipop (**Princess Spotless**)
Tray with seven glasses of gargle (**Duster**)
Dustpan and brush (**Duster**)
Bedtime drink on tray (**Queen**)
Tray of cleansing cream, one glass of gargle (**Auntie Septic**)
Bottle of pills (**Measle**)
Ornate broom (**Grime Minister**)
Rocket Waste Disposal System (**Gadget**)

ACT II

SCENE 1

On stage: Palace throne set as previously, with Rocket System

SCENE 2

Roof set and bedroom corridor, as previously

SCENE 3
Bedroom set and corridor as previously

SCENE 4
Corridor

SCENE 5
Throne room as previously, with Rocket System and Washing
Machine

Off stage: Tray with seven glasses of gargle (**Duster**)
Doctor's bag with thermometer, stethoscope (**Doctor**)
Patent Washing Machine with contents of stiff and shrunken clothes
(**Gadget**)
King's dressing-gown (**Measle**)
Ladder (**Gadget**)
Telephone wire repairing tools, headphones and dial (**Gadget**)
Large hypodermic syringe (**Doctor**)
Telephone tapping device and dial (**Doctor**)
Scissors (**Doctor**)

LIGHTING PLOT

NOTE: The following plot is of essential cues. Extra lighting effects for songs, etc. may be added at the discretion of the producer

Property fittings required: nil
Inside an aeroplane; a throne room; a bedroom and corridor; a roof

ACT I

To open:	House lights on	(Page 1)
Cue 1	At end of first announcement *House lights down*	(Page 1)
Cue 2	**Announcer:** "Thank you" *Houselights out. Bring up interior plane lighting as Curtain rises*	(Page 1)
Cue 3	**Pilot:** ". . . cleanest Kingdom in the world" *Lights become very bright*	(Page 2)
Cue 4	At end of Scene 1 *Fade to Black-Out*	(Page 4)
Cue 5	When ready *Fade up to roof lighting, day*	(Page 4)
Cue 6	At end of Scene 2 *Black-Out*	(Page 8)
Cue 7	When ready *Bring up general lighting on throne room*	(Page 8)
Cue 8	At end of Scene 3 *Fade to Black-Out*	(Page 16)
Cue 9	When ready *Bring up evening lighting on bedroom and corridor*	(Page 16)
Cue 10	**Queen** turns out lights *Reduce room lighting to blue glimmer*	(Page 18)
Cue 11	**Stainless** switches on lights *Return to opening lighting*	(Page 18)
Cue 12	**Spotless:** "I've got SPOTS!" *Fade to Black-Out*	(Page 18)
Cue 13	When ready *Fade up to roof lighting, night*	(Page 19)

ACT II

To open:	General throne room lighting	
Cue 14	**Measle** *exits* *Fade to Black-Out*	(Page 30)
Cue 15	When ready *Fade up to roof lighting, day*	(Page 30)

Cue 16	**King** answers telephone *Bring up spot on telephone on corridor outside bedroom set*	(Page 31)
Cue 17	**King** rings off *Corridor spot off*	(Page 31)
Cue 18	**Doctor** exits *Fade to Black-Out*	(Page 32)
Cue 19	When ready *Fade up on bedroom and corridor*	(Page 32)
Cue 20	**Grime Minister** faints *Cross-fade to roof lighting*	(Page 34)
Cue 21	**Weathervane** dials *Bring up lighting on bedroom and corridor*	(Page 34)
Cue 22	**Weathervane** starts putting telephone wires together *Fade roof lighting to out*	(Page 34)
Cue 23	**Grime Minister:** "Locked!" *Cross-fade to roof lighting*	(Page 36)
Cue 24	**Weathervane** dials *Bring up spot on corridor telephone*	(Page 36)
Cue 25	**Duster** knocks on bedroom door *Bring up bedroom lighting*	(Page 37)
Cue 26	At end of "Hero" song *Fade to Black-Out*	(Page 38)
Cue 27	When ready *Bring up throne room lighting*	(Page 38)
Cue 28	**Spotless** turns off television set *Bring up roof lighting*	(Page 44)

EFFECTS PLOT

ACT I

Cue 1	At end of first announcement *Sound of plane preparing to take off*	(Page 1)
Cue 2	Houselights black out *Plane taking off—continue sound of flight throughout scene and increase, joined by music, at end of scene*	(Page 1)
Cue 3	As CURTAIN rises *Wind effect—repeat at intervals*	(Page 1)
Cue 4	**Weathervane:** ". . . ever happens, nothing . . ." *Sound of plane passing over*	(Page 5)
Cue 5	**Measle** tests phone wires *Bleep bleep from aerial*	(Page 6)
Cue 6	**Measle** dials *Faint telephone ring*	(Page 7)
Cue 7	**Aerial:** ". . . to the throne room" *Bleep bleep from aerial*	(Page 7)
Cue 8	**T.V. Voice:** ". . . . could well be dangerous" *Dramatic chord, and scene change music*	(Page 7)
Cue 9	**Gadget:** ". . . and turner-oner" *Fanfare*	(Page 9)
Cue 10	**Queen:** "That's better" *Clock chimes*	(Page 11)
Cue 11	**Gadget** pushes rocket switch *Sound of engine running—repeat as he switches on and off*	(Page 13)
Cue 12	At end of Rocket song *Rocket whirrs up past window*	(Page 14)
Cue 13	**Gadget:** "Thank you, Auntie Septic" *Bleep bleep from aerial*	(Page 15)
Cue 14	**T.V. Voice:** ". . . . could well be dangerous" *Dramatic chord*	(Page 15)
Cue 15	**King:** "Come, my dear" *Music for Court exit*	(Page 16)
Cue 16	**Princess Spotless** exits *Tension music*	(Page 16)
Cue 17	**Princess Spotless:** "I've got SPOTS!" *Telephone rings*	(Page 18)
Cue 18	**Aerial:** ". . . we're edgy, all this . . ." *Bleep bleep from aerial*	(Page 19)
Cue 19	**Measle:** "Mission B accomplished" *Sudden gust of wind*	(Page 20)

ACT II

MADE AND PRINTED IN GREAT BRITAIN BY
LATIMER TREND & COMPANY LTD PLYMOUTH
MADE IN ENGLAND